The Usborne
First
Encyclopedia
of
History

Fiona Chandler

Designed by Susie McCaffrey

Illustrated by David Hancock

Consultants: Dr. Anne Millard
and Dr. David Martill

Using Internet links

Throughout this book we have recommended websites where you can find out more about history. To visit the sites, go to the **Usborne Quicklinks Website** where you will find links to all the sites.

1. Go to **www.usborne-quicklinks.com**
2. Type the keywords for this book:
first history
3. Type the page number of the link you want to visit.
4. Click on the link to go to the recommended site.

Here are some of the things you can do on the websites recommended in this book:

• Make dinosaur models and print out fact cards
• Write your name like a Babylonian
• Join Stone Age people in their cave
• Explore inside an Egyptian pyramid

Site availability

The links in Usborne Quicklinks are regularly reviewed and updated, but occasionally you may get a message that a site is unavailable. This might be temporary, so try again later, or even the next day. Websites do occasionally close down and when this happens, we will replace them with new links in Usborne Quicklinks. Sometimes we add extra links too, if we think they are useful. So when you visit Usborne Quicklinks, the links may be slightly different from those described in your book.

Downloadable pictures

Pictures marked with a * in this book can be downloaded from the Usborne Quicklinks Website. These pictures are for personal use only and must not be used for commercial purposes.

COMPUTER NOT ESSENTIAL
If you don't have access to the Internet, don't worry. This book is a fun and informative introduction to history on its own.

Safety on the Internet

Ask your parent's or guardian's permission before you connect to the Internet and make sure you follow these simple rules:

• Never give out information about yourself, such as your real name, address, phone number or the name of your school.

• If a site asks you to log in or register by typing your name or email address, ask permission from an adult first.

What you need

To visit the websites you need a computer with an Internet connection and a web browser (the software that lets you look at information from the Internet). Some sites need extra programs (plug-ins) to play sound or show videos or animations.

If you go to a site and do not have the necessary plug-in, a message will come up on the screen. There is usually a link to click on to download the plug-in. For more information about plug-ins, go to Usborne Quicklinks and click on "Net Help".

Notes for parents and guardians

The websites described in this book are regularly reviewed, but the content of a website may change at any time and Usborne Publishing is not responsible for the content on any website other than its own.

We recommend that children are supervised while on the Internet, that they do not use Internet chat rooms, and that you use Internet filtering software to block unsuitable material. Please ensure that your children read and follow the safety guidelines printed above. For more information, see the Net Help area on the Usborne Quicklinks Website.

Contents

This is an Ancient Egyptian wall painting. It shows a nobleman hunting birds.

There were animals on Earth long before there were any people. Different kinds of animals lived at different times. At one time, the biggest and fastest animals on Earth were the dinosaurs.

There were many kinds of dinosaurs. Here you can see one of the biggest and one of the smallest compared with a person.

★

Internet link

For a link to a website where you can explore the world of the dinosaurs, go to **www.usborne-quicklinks.com**

What were dinosaurs?

Dinosaurs belonged to a group of animals called reptiles. All reptiles have scaly skin. Birds also have some scaly skin, and experts think they are probably a kind of dinosaur too.

All dinosaurs lived on land. Some hunted other animals for food, but many of them ate plants. Most dinosaurs died out 65 million years ago, long before the first people appeared. Only the birds survived.

Baby dinosaurs grew inside eggs laid by their mothers. These babies have just broken out of their eggs. This is called hatching.

Diplodocus was a huge, plant-eating dinosaur. It was longer than two buses placed end to end.

Sea and sky

At the time of the dinosaurs, there were also lots of flying reptiles in the sky. They were called pterosaurs (say "terra-sors"). Other huge reptiles swam in the sea.

This is Triceratops (say "try-ser-a-tops"). It had horns for fighting off attackers.

This sea reptile is called an ichthyosaur (say "ick-thee-oh-sor"). It was a powerful swimmer.

Pterosaurs had big, leathery wings. This is a pterosaur called Pteranodon (say "ter-ran-oh-don").

Tyrannosaurus rex was taller than an elephant.

This dinosaur had long, sharp teeth for tearing up meat.

This fierce dinosaur is called Tyrannosaurus rex (say "tie-ran-oh-saw-russ rex"). It was a meat-eater.

Claws for holding onto food

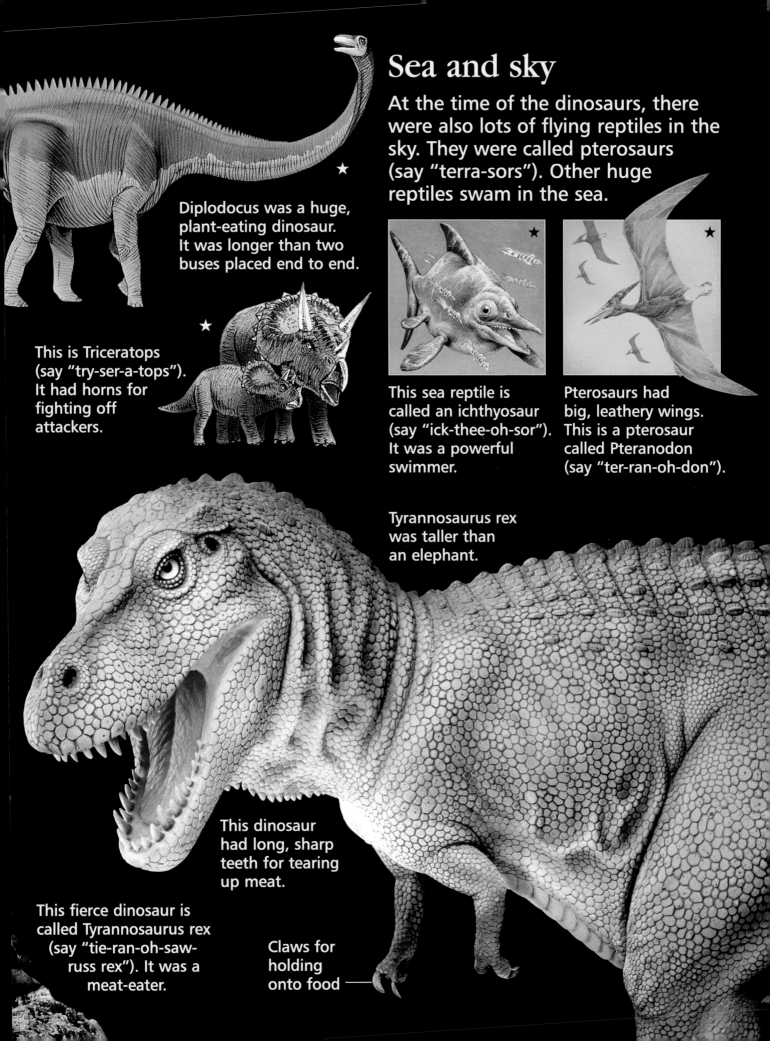

The first people

The first people lived by hunting animals, catching fish and gathering plants to eat. As the seasons changed, they moved around from place to place looking for food.

In the summer, people lived in tents that they made from branches and animal skins.

In the winter, when it was cold, they sometimes sheltered in caves.

Finding food

People spent a lot of time looking for food. They hunted deer, horses, bison and wild pigs for meat. They also ate whatever plants and small animals they could find.

These are some of the things that the first people ate.

Fish

Berries

Snails

Dandelion leaves

Nuts

Mushrooms

Crabs

Birds' eggs

Shellfish

Lizards

These animals were painted on the wall of a cave at Lascaux, in France. Can you guess what kinds of animals they are meant to be? (Answer on page 64.)

Cave paintings

Inside the deepest, darkest caves, people painted pictures of the animals they hunted. They may have thought that the pictures were magical and would help them with their hunting.

Internet link

For a link to a website where you can see lots more cave paintings, go to **www.usborne-quicklinks.com**

Stone tools

The first people used tools made from a kind of stone called flint. They used spears tipped with a sharp, flint point for hunting. They also made flint axes and knives for cutting up meat.

Later, people made arrows with flint tips like this.

The first farmers

Farming began when people learned how to plant seeds to grow food. They also tamed animals, such as sheep and cows. This meant that people could stay in one place, instead of moving around to find food.

This clay pot was made by early farmers in Turkey.

Growing food

Around 12,000 years ago, people in the Middle East began growing wheat and barley. They ground the grain into flour for making bread.

These are wheat plants. You can see the grains at the top of each stalk.

Making things

Farmers didn't need to spend all day looking for food, so they had time to learn new things. They made clay pots for storing and cooking food.

They also learned how to make cloth by spinning and weaving wool.

This is part of a farming village in the Middle East. It has a wall around it to keep out wild animals.

This man is offering gifts to a statue of the village goddess.

New tools

The first farmers made tools from stone, bone and wood. Later, people learned how to make things from metal. The first metal tools were made of copper.

This is a sickle. It was used for cutting crops.

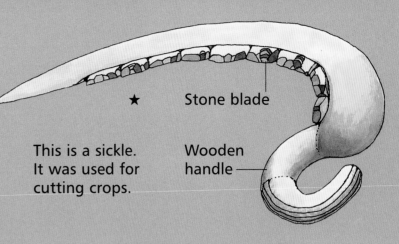

★ Stone blade

Wooden handle

Women carry water from the stream.

People use tools called sickles to cut the crops.

These men are making mud bricks to mend the wall.

The roofs of the houses are covered with straw.

Cows are kept for their meat, milk and skins.

The first cities

Small farming villages gradually grew into big, crowded cities. Some of the first cities in the world were in the Middle East, in an area called Sumer.

Living in a city

Each city had a wall around it to keep out enemies. Inside the city, there were houses, schools, and workshops for making things. There was a temple too, where people took gifts for the city's god.

This golden helmet came from a city called Ur. It was found in the grave of a dead king.

This is a city in Sumer. You can see people going in a procession to the temple.

Temple wall

The temple is built on a big, stepped platform, called a ziggurat.

School

Soldiers

Potter's workshop

The first wheels

About 5,500 years ago, potters in Sumer began using a wheel to shape their pots. These were the first wheels in the world. Later, the Sumerians used wheels on carts and chariots.

Wheels were made from three pieces of wood joined together.

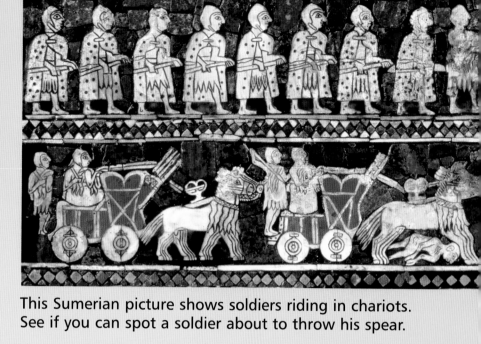

This Sumerian picture shows soldiers riding in chariots. See if you can spot a soldier about to throw his spear.

★

Internet link

For a link to a website where you can write your name in Ancient Sumerian, go to **www.usborne-quicklinks.com**

Tablets and seals

★

Most people couldn't read or write, so they hired a man called a scribe. Scribes wrote on pieces of wet clay, called tablets. These were then baked hard in an oven.

Reed pen

Clay tablet

People used stone seals to sign things. They rolled the seal onto soft clay, leaving a picture behind.

★

Rolling a seal

Picture on clay

The houses have flat roofs.

Board game

These men are making weapons from metal.

11

Ancient Egypt

The Ancient Egyptians were farmers who lived along the banks of the Nile. They used water from the river to help them grow food. The Egyptians were ruled by a powerful king called a pharaoh.

Internet link

For a link to a website where you can explore inside the Great Pyramid, go to
www.usborne-quicklinks.com

A gold mask from the tomb of the pharaoh Tutankhamun

Pharaohs and pyramids

Some pharaohs were buried inside huge, stone pyramids on the edge of the desert. The pharaoh's body was placed in a secret room in the middle of the pyramid. There are still about 80 pyramids in Egypt, and each one took at least 20 years to build.

These are the pyramids at Giza. Three pharaohs and their wives were buried here.

A pharaoh called Menkaure was buried inside this pyramid.

This is the Great Pyramid. It is made up of over two million stone blocks.

Menkaure's three wives were buried in these smaller pyramids.

Mummies and coffins

The Egyptians tried to stop dead people's bodies from rotting away. They thought this would allow them to have another life after they died. They took out the person's insides, dried the body out and wrapped it in bandages. Bodies kept like this are called mummies.

The insides of the body were kept in jars like these.

Mummies were put inside painted wooden coffins like this one.

Picture writing

Egyptian writing was made up of lots of small pictures, or symbols, called hieroglyphs (say "hi-ro-gliffs"). There were over 700 different symbols. Here are just a few of them:

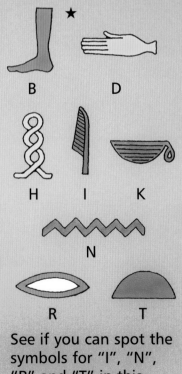

★ B   D

H   I   K

N

R   T

See if you can spot the symbols for "I", "N", "R" and "T" in this Egyptian painting.

13

Celtic warriors

The people we call the Celts lived in most parts of western Europe. They were fierce warriors, but they were also great poets, artists and musicians.

The Celts made beautiful metal objects decorated with curves and spirals. This is the back of a Celtic mirror.

Forts and fighting

The Celts lived in big groups, called tribes. Different tribes often fought each other. Chiefs built forts on hill tops to keep their families safe from enemies. The forts were surrounded by ditches and big mounds of earth. This made them very hard to attack.

These are the remains of a Celtic hillfort. You can still see the ditches and mounds around the hill top.

Here are some Celtic warriors charging into battle.

The warriors yell loudly to scare their enemies.

War trumpets make a terrifying noise.

Nobles ride in wooden chariots.

Some of the warriors have painted blue patterns on their bodies to make themselves look scary.

Home life

The Celts lived in big, round houses. Inside, there was just one room, where the whole family cooked, ate and slept. Chiefs and their families had houses inside a hillfort. Everyone else lived in small villages.

This roundhouse belongs to a chief. He and his warriors are having a feast to celebrate winning a battle.

The roof is covered with straw.

The walls are made of twigs plastered with mud and straw.

Straw mattress for sleeping on

People wear clothes with bright checks and stripes.

A poet, called a bard, chants poems about Celtic heroes.

Wild boar roasting on a spit

People drink from hollowed-out animal horns.

Internet link

For a link to a website where you can watch a roundhouse being built, go to **www.usborne-quicklinks.com**

All the warriors have strong iron weapons.

Gods and priests

The Celts believed that some of their gods lived in streams, rocks and trees. Celtic priests, called druids, threw precious things into lakes and rivers as gifts to the gods.

A druid dropping a sword into a pool

15

Ancient Greece

In ancient times, Greece wasn't all one country like it is today. Instead, each city had its own rulers. The greatest of these cities was Athens, which was famous for its learning and plays.

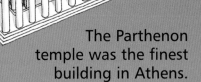

The Parthenon temple was the finest building in Athens.

Big buildings

In every city in Greece, people built huge, stone temples for their gods and goddesses. Greek temples usually had a triangular-shaped roof held up by rows of tall pillars.

These are the ruins of the Parthenon temple. It stands on a hill high above the city of Athens.

Spot the pillar

The Greeks used three types of pillars in their buildings. Can you spot which type they used for the Parthenon?

A Doric pillar ★

An Ionic pillar ★

A Corinthian pillar ★

The walls and pillars are made from a stone called marble.

This is how big people look compared with the Parthenon.

The first plays

The first great plays in the world were written by the Ancient Greeks. They believed that performing the plays would please their gods. People put the plays on at festivals which lasted several days. There was a prize for the best play.

Internet link

For a link to a website where you can visit the Ancient Olympic Games and watch a Greek play, go to **www.usborne-quicklinks.com**

Actors playing gods can fly through the air on this crane.

Musicians

Scenery

Stage

★ Here you can see Greek actors putting on a play at a festival.

The Olympic Games

The Greeks loved athletics and they organized competitions all over the country. The most famous was the Olympic Games, which took place every four years at Olympia.

The actors wear masks and costumes to show which parts they are playing.

These actors are called the chorus. They perform songs and dances to explain what is happening on the stage.

This Greek painting shows an athlete training for the long jump.

Ancient China

From about 2,200 years ago, China was ruled by powerful emperors. The first emperor was called Qin Shi Huangdi (say "chin shee hwong-dee").

Internet link

For a link to a website where you can explore the Great Wall of China, go to **www.usborne-quicklinks.com**

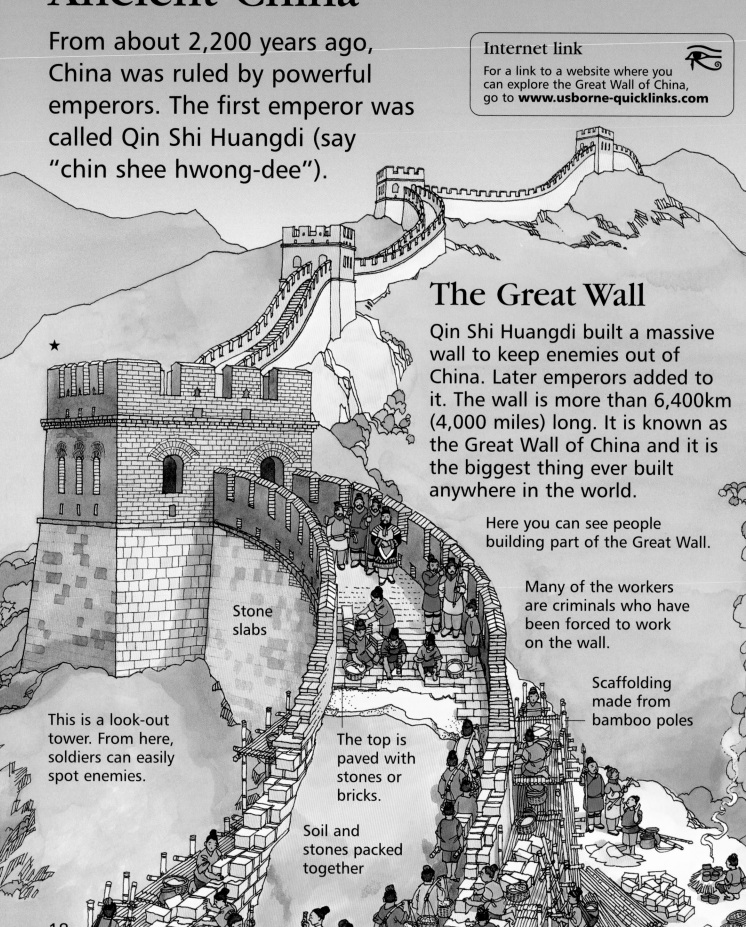

The Great Wall

Qin Shi Huangdi built a massive wall to keep enemies out of China. Later emperors added to it. The wall is more than 6,400km (4,000 miles) long. It is known as the Great Wall of China and it is the biggest thing ever built anywhere in the world.

Here you can see people building part of the Great Wall.

Many of the workers are criminals who have been forced to work on the wall.

Stone slabs

Scaffolding made from bamboo poles

This is a look-out tower. From here, soldiers can easily spot enemies.

The top is paved with stones or bricks.

Soil and stones packed together

Growing food

Most people in China were farmers. In the north, they grew wheat and a kind of grain called millet. In the south, the weather was warmer and wetter. There, farmers grew rice in flooded fields, called paddy fields.

These women are planting rice shoots. Chinese farmers have been growing rice in this way for 7,000 years.

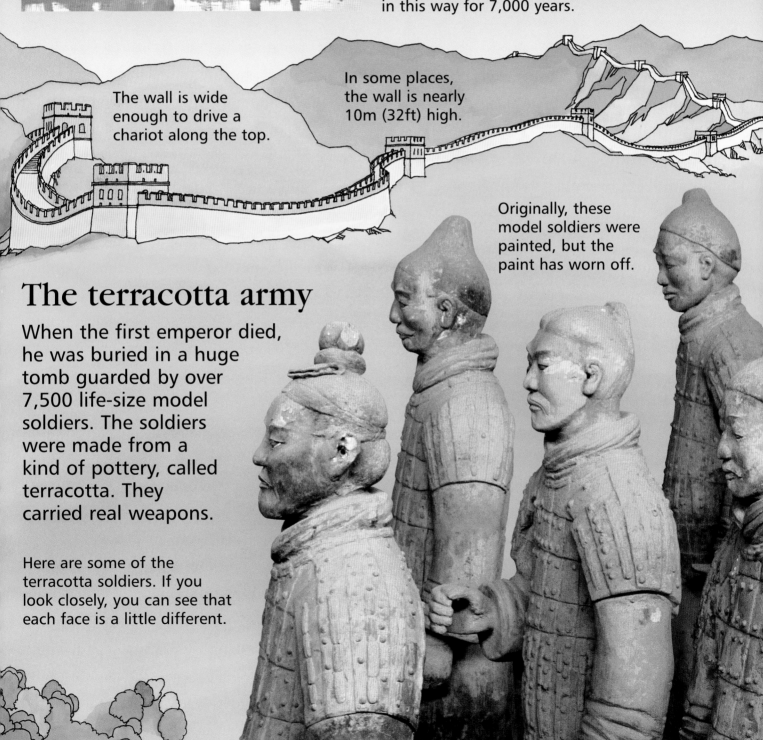

The wall is wide enough to drive a chariot along the top.

In some places, the wall is nearly 10m (32ft) high.

Originally, these model soldiers were painted, but the paint has worn off.

The terracotta army

When the first emperor died, he was buried in a huge tomb guarded by over 7,500 life-size model soldiers. The soldiers were made from a kind of pottery, called terracotta. They carried real weapons.

Here are some of the terracotta soldiers. If you look closely, you can see that each face is a little different.

Ancient Rome

About 2,000 years ago, Rome was one of the biggest cities in the world. At that time, the Romans ruled all the lands around the Mediterranean Sea. These lands were called the Roman Empire.

On this map, all the lands shown in red were once part of the Roman Empire.

Roman soldiers wore iron helmets and carried wooden shields.

The Roman army

The Romans had a huge army of well-trained soldiers. They used their army to fight for new lands and to protect the Empire from enemies. Most soldiers fought on foot using a spear, a sword and a dagger.

Roman soldiers built long, straight roads linking towns all over the Empire.

Internet link

For a link to a website with information, activities and fun facts about the Romans, go to **www.usborne-quicklinks.com**

Home comforts

In Rome, rich people lived in comfortable houses with large gardens. Some houses even had toilets, running water and a kind of central heating.

This is a Roman house. Parts of it have been cut away so you can see inside.

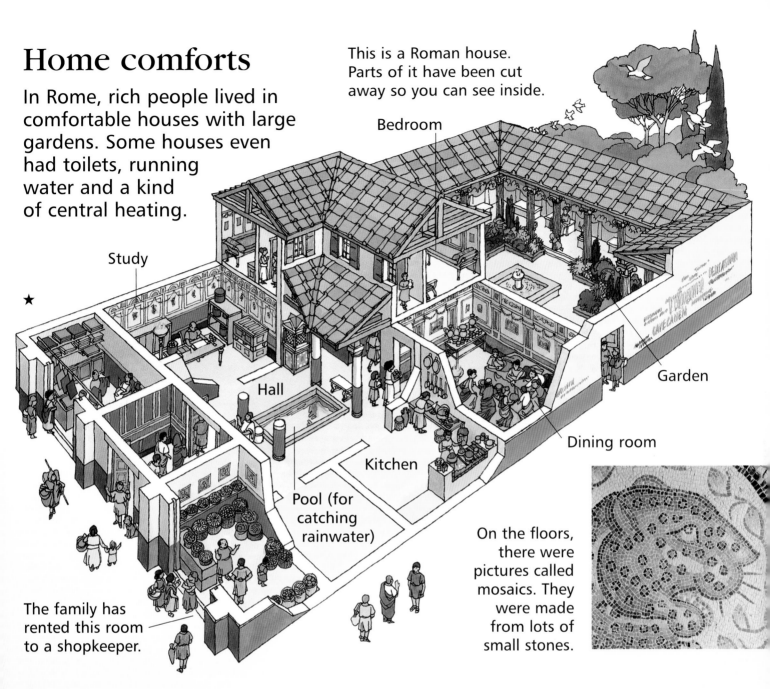

Bedroom

Study

Hall

Kitchen

Pool (for catching rainwater)

Garden

Dining room

The family has rented this room to a shopkeeper.

On the floors, there were pictures called mosaics. They were made from lots of small stones.

Roman pastimes

The Romans loved watching chariot races. These took place at a huge racetrack called a circus.

People also enjoyed watching gladiators fight each other. Gladiators often died in these brutal fights.

Most Romans went to the public baths every day to relax, exercise, meet friends – and to get themselves clean.

1,200 years ago

Viking raiders

The Vikings came from Norway, Sweden and Denmark. They were great sailors and traders, but they were also fierce warriors. They attacked and robbed villages all around the coasts of Europe.

This man is dressed as a Viking warrior.

A Viking longship

Greenland
Iceland
North America
British Isles
France
Spain
Italy
The Vikings lived here.

The Vikings sailed to all these places.

Viking ships

The Vikings made their attacks in fast boats, called longships. The ships were strong enough to sail across rough seas. They weren't very deep, so they could also travel up shallow rivers.

This carved dragon's head is meant to scare enemies.

The Vikings in this ship are on their way to launch a raid.

There's a big oar at the back for steering the ship.

Viking homes

Viking chiefs lived in large homes called longhouses. Each longhouse had only one big room, where everyone ate, worked and slept. There weren't any windows, so it must have been very dark inside.

Part of this longhouse has been cut away so you can see inside.

A hole in the roof lets out smoke from the fire.

The chief's bedroom

This woman is weaving cloth using a wooden frame called a loom.

The roof is covered with straw.

The walls are made of logs.

Toilet

Most people sleep on benches at the sides of the room.

In the winter, farm animals are kept inside.

Women used brooches like this to fasten their clothes.

Internet link

For a link to a website where you can have fun spotting the things that don't belong in a Viking house, go to
www.usborne-quicklinks.com

Viking crafts

The Vikings made beautiful brooches, arm rings and belt buckles from gold, silver and bronze. They also carved spoons and combs from pieces of animal bone and horn.

23

African kingdoms

Africa is an enormous continent with hot, sandy deserts, thick forests and huge, grassy plains. Each area had its own way of life. In some places, rich kingdoms grew up.

The people of Benin, in West Africa, made beautiful bronze statues like this.

★

Traders from North Africa used camels to get across the Sahara Desert to Mali.

Kingdom of gold

In Mali, in West Africa, people dug gold out of the ground. Traders came from North Africa to buy the gold, and Mali became very rich.

These are some of the things the traders bought and sold.

Ivory (elephants' tusks)

★

Gold

Salt

Walls made of mud bricks

The North African traders were Muslims, and many people in Mali became Muslims too. Cities in Mali had big buildings, called mosques, where Muslims could pray. There were also Muslim schools and universities.

This is the Grand Mosque in Djenne, in Mali. The original mosque fell into ruins, but this one was built in the same style.

Stone city

In the grasslands of southern Africa was the city of Great Zimbabwe. Its people grew rich by trading gold and copper. The king lived inside a walled fortress in the middle of the city.

Internet link

For a link to a website where you can go on a treasure hunt around Africa, go to **www.usborne-quicklinks.com**

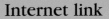

This is the fortress at Great Zimbabwe.

This tower is made of stones. It is solid all the way through.

People take part in religious ceremonies here.

The houses are built of clay and gravel.

Grass roof

The walls are made of stone blocks. There are nearly a million of them in the outside wall.

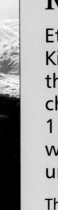

Rock churches

Ethiopia was a Christian kingdom. King Lalibela of Ethiopia believed that God had told him to carve churches out of solid rock. He built 11 churches like this. Some of them were linked together by tunnels under the ground.

This is one of King Lalibela's churches. All of them were carved in the shape of a cross.

Living in a castle

In the Middle Ages (between 500 and 1,000 years ago) kings and lords in Europe often fought each other for land. They built castles with strong, stone walls to protect themselves from their enemies.

Inside a castle

A lord lived in a castle with his family and all his soldiers and servants. It must have been very cold inside, because the first castles had no glass in the windows.

This picture shows part of a castle. Some of the walls have been cut away to let you see inside.

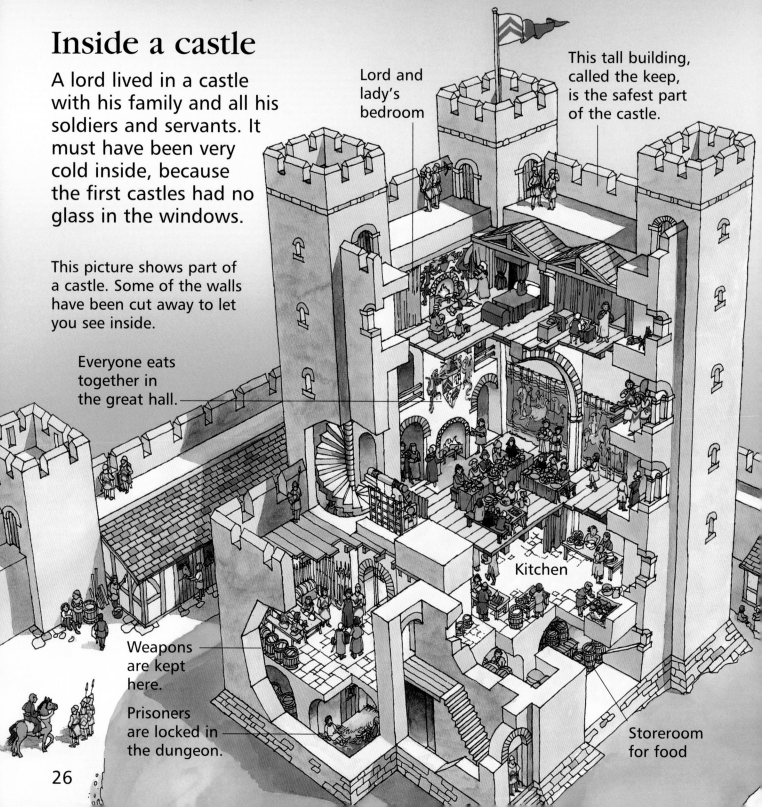

Lord and lady's bedroom

This tall building, called the keep, is the safest part of the castle.

Everyone eats together in the great hall.

Kitchen

Weapons are kept here.

Prisoners are locked in the dungeon.

Storeroom for food

Noble knights

Knights were soldiers who fought on horseback. Only boys from noble families could train to be knights. A good knight had to be strong and brave. He also had to promise to fight only for his lord.

This picture from the Middle Ages shows two knights taking part in a contest called a joust.

Painted shield

Chainmail shirt made from lots of metal rings

This knight is being knocked off his horse.

This long spear is called a lance.

Internet link

For a link to a website where you can explore a castle and meet the people who lived there, go to **www.usborne-quicklinks.com**

This wall keeps enemies out.

Guards look out for enemies.

Fun feasts

Feasts took place in the great hall of the castle. The guests ate lots of rich food, such as roast swan, spiced beef, squirrel stew and sugared mackerel. For dessert, there might be apple pie or honey cakes.

A jester told jokes to make the guests laugh.

Musicians, called minstrels, played their instruments and sang.

Living in a village

In the Middle Ages, most people in Europe were farmers who lived in small villages. The land around each village belonged to a lord. All the villagers lived and worked on the lord's land.

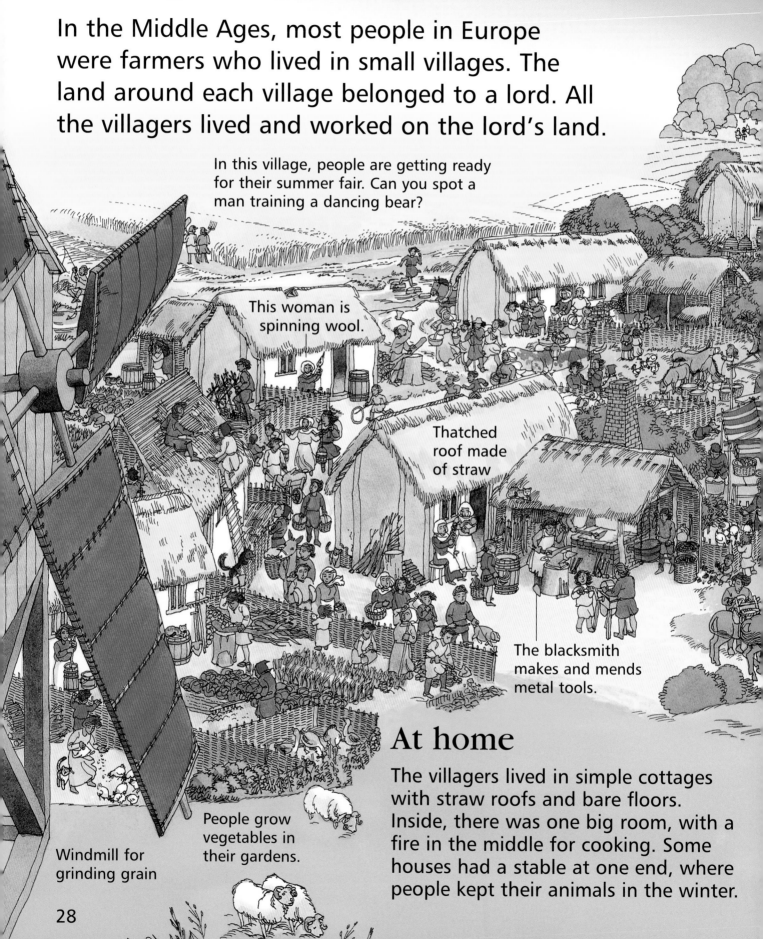

In this village, people are getting ready for their summer fair. Can you spot a man training a dancing bear?

This woman is spinning wool.

Thatched roof made of straw

The blacksmith makes and mends metal tools.

Windmill for grinding grain

People grow vegetables in their gardens.

At home

The villagers lived in simple cottages with straw roofs and bare floors. Inside, there was one big room, with a fire in the middle for cooking. Some houses had a stable at one end, where people kept their animals in the winter.

The lord lived in a castle or in a big house, called a manor house. The picture on the right shows a manor house in southern England.

Everyone goes to church on Sundays.

In the fields

Most villages had three big fields. Each family had a few strips of land in each field. People planted wheat and barley in two of the fields. Every year, they left one field unplanted to let the soil rest and get back its goodness.

This picture from the Middle Ages shows a farmer cutting his crops with a tool called a sickle.

The Black Death

In 1347, a terrible illness spread to Europe from Asia. It was called the Black Death, because sick people got black spots on their bodies. Millions died. In some villages, no one was left alive.

The Black Death was spread by fleas living on rats like this one.

Internet link

For a link to a website with games and more about life in the Middle Ages, go to **www.usborne-quicklinks.com**

29

Inca cities

The Incas lived in the Andes mountains of South America. Most of them were farmers, but they were also great builders. They were ruled by an emperor called the Inca.

These people are acting out an old Inca festival at the city of Cuzco, in Peru.

Cities of stone

The Incas built huge cities from massive blocks of stone. They used stone hammers to shape the blocks so they would fit together perfectly. Each city had temples, palaces, and observatories for watching the stars.

Machu Picchu is 2,350m (7,700ft) above sea level.

This is the ruined Inca city of Machu Picchu, high up in the Andes mountains.

On the road

The Incas built stone roads to link their cities together. Teams of runners used the roads to carry messages from city to city. The roads were also used by soldiers, traders, and farmers taking food to market.

Llamas were used for carrying heavy loads.

The Incas made bridges out of reeds, so people could get across valleys and rivers.

Food and drink

Inca farmers grew corn, potatoes, peppers, beans, tomatoes and squash. They kept guinea pigs for their meat. Women made a drink called chicha by spitting chewed fruit into warm water.

Internet link

For a link to a website where you can investigate an Inca city, go to **www.usborne-quicklinks.com**

★ Squash

★ Peppers

★ Tomatoes

★ Beans

★ Corn

Farmers grew food on wide ledges, called terraces, that they dug into the mountainside.

31

Aztec life

The Aztecs lived in what is now Mexico. They were fierce warriors and were often at war with other groups of people nearby. Winning wars gave the Aztecs lots of new land and they became very powerful.

This scary mask shows the face of an Aztec god named Quetzalcoatl.

The best Aztec warriors were the Eagle knights and Jaguar knights.

Eagle knight

Jaguar knight

Island city

The Aztecs' capital city was called Tenochtitlán. It was built on some islands near the edge of Lake Texcoco. The islands were joined to the mainland by raised roads. In the middle of the city was a huge square filled with temples.

This picture shows part of the square in the middle of Tenochtitlán.

This is a school for priests. Only boys can go here.

Here, people play a ball game called tlatchtli. The game is part of the Aztec religion.

Canal

Market

Wooden bridge

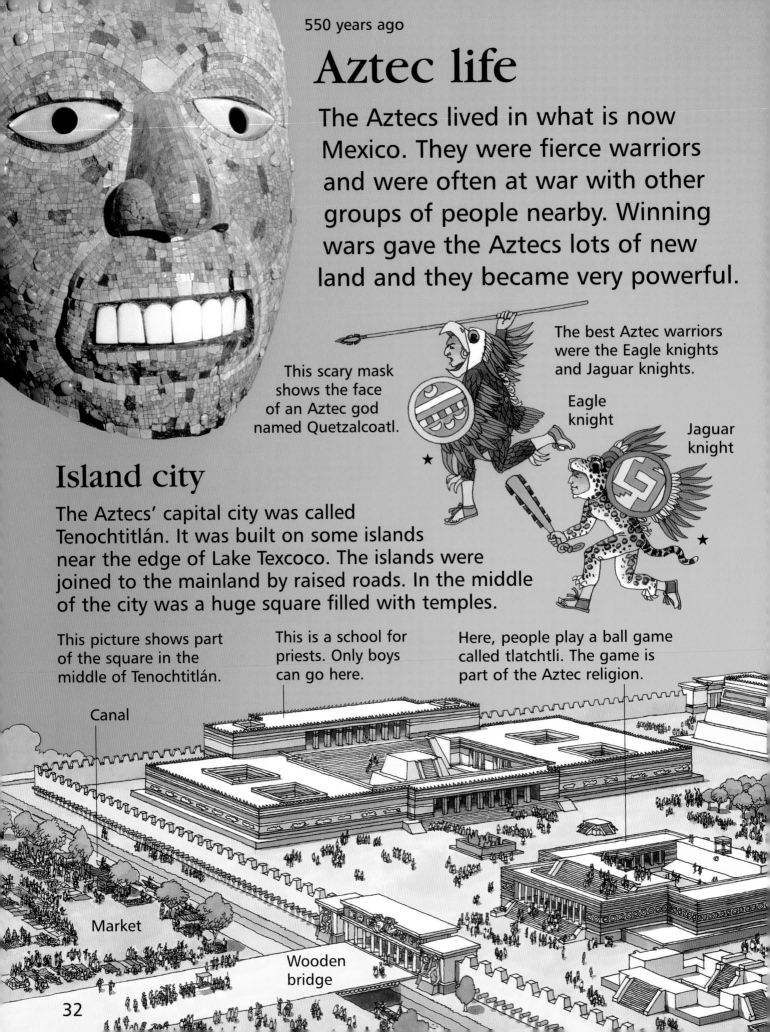

Gifts for a god

The Aztecs believed that their sun god needed human hearts to keep him alive. Every year, Aztec priests killed thousands of people and gave their hearts to the god. Most of the people who died like this were enemies who were captured in war.

This is the sun god Huitzilopochtli. He is holding a shield and a magic weapon, called the Fire Serpent.

Digging stick

Farmers digging the soil in their floating fields

Floating fields

In the lake all around Tenochtitlán, farmers grew food in huge, floating fields. The fields were like giant baskets filled with mud and soil. People grew corn, beans, tomatoes and peppers. They used the corn to bake thin pancakes, called tortillas.

Internet link

For a link to a website with pictures, information and quizzes about the Aztecs, go to **www.usborne-quicklinks.com**

Temple of Huitzilopochtli, the god of sun and war

Temple of Quetzalcoatl, the snake god

The temples are built on top of tall pyramids.

Temple of Tlaloc, the rain god

33

Italian ideas

In Italy, people began to study the art and learning of Ancient Greece and Rome. Artists, thinkers and scientists tried out new ideas based on what they had learned. This exciting time is known as the Renaissance.

Rich people, called patrons, paid artists to create paintings and statues for them.

Beautiful buildings

Architects studied the ruins of Roman buildings to find out how they were built. Then they designed elegant new buildings in the same style, with pillars, domes and rounded arches.

This is Florence Cathedral in Italy. Its huge dome was one of the first examples of the new Renaissance style.

The dome took 16 years to build. It is made from over four million bricks.

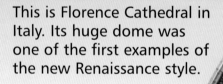

Internet link

For a link to a website with a fun introduction to the Renaissance, go to **www.usborne-quicklinks.com**

The dome of Florence Cathedral is really two domes joined together, one inside the other. This makes it very strong.

Outer dome ——

Inner dome

Perfect pictures

Artists found new ways to make their paintings more realistic. They realized that things that are far away look smaller than things that are close up. This is called perspective. It gives pictures a feeling of depth and distance.

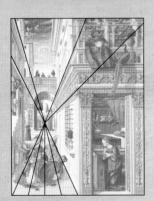

In this painting, can you see how the people get smaller the farther away they are?

All the straight lines meet at a single point in the distance.

This is part of a painting called *The Birth of Venus*, by Sandro Botticelli. The artist used light and shade to make Venus look solid.

Science and inventions

Scientists studied plants, animals and people, and did experiments to test out new ideas. Inventors worked on new designs for clocks, weapons, water pumps, and other machines.

These machines were designed by a man named Leonardo da Vinci. Most of his machines were never built.

This is a tank. Inside it, four men would have turned the wheels to push it along.

A helicopter

Exploring the world

In Europe, spices and silks from India and China were very popular – and very expensive. They had to be carried over land on long, dangerous journeys. Europeans began looking for ways to the East by sea.

Ginger

Cinnamon

Spices from the East

Pepper

Nutmeg

This is an explorers' ship. Parts of it have been cut away so you can see inside.

Life at sea

Sailors look out for land from the crow's nest.

Explorers had to be brave. They sailed for months at a time and had no idea when they would find land. Lots of sailors got sick and died because they had no fresh fruit or vegetables to eat. Many ships were wrecked in storms and never returned.

Sailors climb ropes to put up the sails.

Captain's cabin

These animals will be killed and eaten on the journey.

The ship is 30m (100ft) long – about as long as three buses.

This is the rudder. It is used for steering the ship.

Barrels of food and water

Around the world

Many people in Europe believed that the Earth was flat, but some thought it was round like a ball. An Italian explorer, named Christopher Columbus, was sure he could reach India by sailing west and going all the way around the world. He set out from Spain and headed across the Atlantic Ocean.

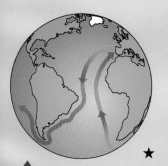

In 1492, Christopher Columbus reached the West Indies. He thought he had made it to India.

Vasco da Gama was the first European to find a way to India by sea. He sailed around Africa.

Ferdinand Magellan's ship was the first to sail around the world. This proved that the Earth was round.

Columbus found coconut palms and other plants that weren't known in Europe.

Finding the way

There were no maps of the oceans, so sailors had to find their own way across. They had only a few simple instruments to help them.

This is an astrolabe. Sailors used it to figure out how far north or south they were.

This is a compass. Sailors used it to find out which way their ship was heading.

Internet link

For a link to a website where you can have dinner on board Columbus's ship, go to
www.usborne-quicklinks.com

Tudor England

The Tudors were a family of kings and queens. They ruled England for over a hundred years and made the country rich and powerful.

This is a painting of King Henry VIII. He divorced two of his wives and had two of them beheaded.

These coins came from the wreck of a Tudor warship.

Henry VIII

Henry VIII became king when he was 17 years old. He married six times, but only had three children. Henry had an argument with the Pope (the head of the Church in Europe) and set up his own English Church.

Internet link

For links to websites where you can find out more about the Tudors, go to **www.usborne-quicklinks.com**

Explorers and pirates

In Tudor times, many explorers sailed to North and South America. They brought back new foods, such as potatoes. Some English explorers were pirates too. They stole treasure from Spanish ships on the coast of America.

Elizabeth I

Queen Elizabeth was the last and greatest of the Tudors. She ruled England for 45 years. During her reign, England fought off an attack by a group of Spanish ships, called the Spanish Armada.

This is a portrait of Elizabeth. She loved clothes and owned 260 different dresses.

Plays and playhouses

In Elizabeth's time, people loved going to see plays. In London, actors performed in playhouses such as the Globe. The most popular plays were written by William Shakespeare.

Here you can see actors performing a play at the Globe.

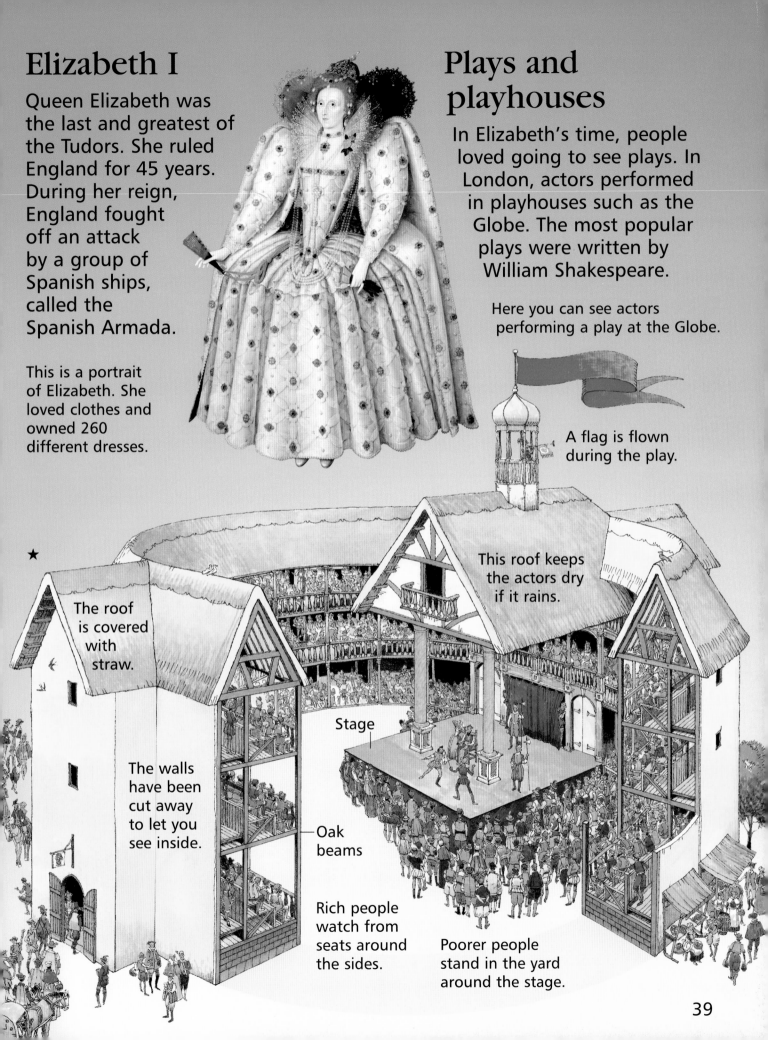

A flag is flown during the play.

This roof keeps the actors dry if it rains.

The roof is covered with straw.

The walls have been cut away to let you see inside.

Stage

Oak beams

Rich people watch from seats around the sides.

Poorer people stand in the yard around the stage.

The Chinese invented gunpowder. They used it for making fireworks, as well as weapons.

Ming China

Around 500 years ago, China was ruled by a family of emperors called the Ming. The Ming emperors made Beijing their capital city. They lived there in a huge palace, called the Forbidden City.

The Forbidden City

The Forbidden City was made up of great halls, temples, courtyards and gardens. It was surrounded by a wall and a moat (a big ditch filled with water). Only the emperor's family and servants were allowed inside.

In this picture, you can see a royal procession outside the Hall of Supreme Harmony in the Forbidden City.

The buildings are made of wood and bricks glued together with steamed rice and egg whites.

The palace has 9,999 rooms and is as big as 74 soccer fields. It took a million workers 14 years to build.

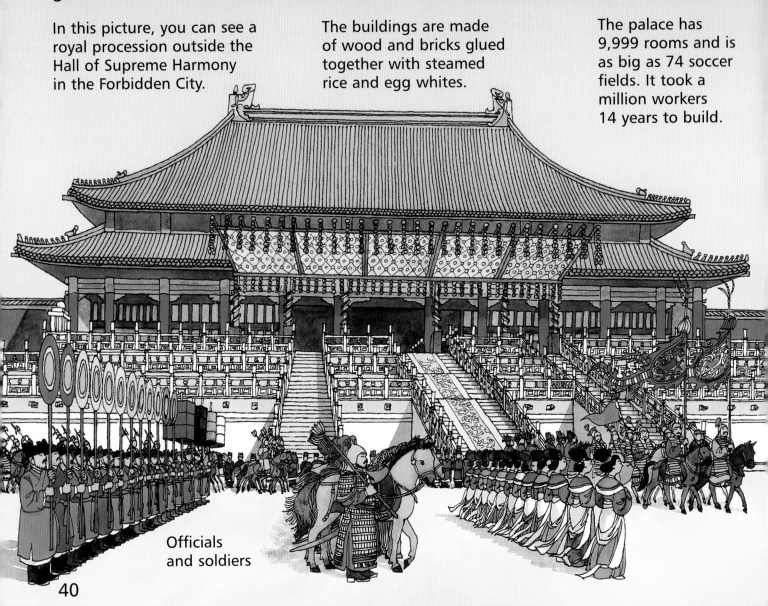

Officials and soldiers

Made in China

In Ming times, the Chinese made many beautiful things. They are especially famous for making a kind of fine pottery, called porcelain. They also made a very expensive kind of cloth, called silk.

Porcelain jar

This wooden box is covered with a shiny varnish called lacquer.

This picture was painted on silk. It shows two Chinese officials.

Internet link

For a link to a website where you can look around the Forbidden City, go to **www.usborne-quicklinks.com**

Time for tea

The Chinese started growing tea about 1,700 years ago. At first, they used the leaves to make medicines. Later, tea became a very popular drink. The Chinese made their tea in teapots and drank it out of little bowls.

Chinese workers picking leaves from tea plants

The emperor rides in a coach pulled by elephants.

Russian rulers

For hundreds of years, Russia was ruled by powerful emperors, called tsars. The tsars wanted to make Russia bigger and stronger, but some of them treated their people very badly.

This is Tsar Ivan the Terrible. He got his name because he enjoyed hurting and killing people.

Russian religion

The Russians were Christians and their Church was called the Orthodox Church. As well as running the country, the tsar had to carry out lots of religious ceremonies. Many tsars also built beautiful churches which you can still see today.

This is St. Basil's Cathedral in Moscow. It was built by Tsar Ivan the Terrible to celebrate winning a war.

The cathedral is made up of nine small churches joined together.

The walls are made of brick and are covered with bright tiles.

Domes shaped like this are called onion domes.

The pointed roofs are called tent roofs.

Peter the Great

Tsar Peter the Great turned Russia into a modern European country. He built canals, ships and factories, and started a navy. He also built a new capital city, called St. Petersburg, on the shores of the Baltic Sea.

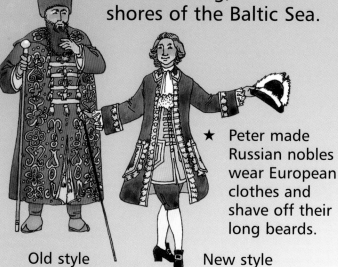

★ Peter made Russian nobles wear European clothes and shave off their long beards.

Old style   New style

This is Peter the Great's Summer Palace, near St. Petersburg. It has over 140 fountains with nearly 22km (14 miles) of water pipes.

Internet link

For a link to a website where you can watch video clips of the Summer Palace, go to **www.usborne-quicklinks.com**

Village life

Most Russians lived in small villages in the countryside. Some people were well off, but most were very poor. Many of them were serfs. Serfs had to work in one place and weren't allowed to change jobs. If the land where they worked was sold, the serfs were sold too.

Here you can see part of a Russian village.

Church

People get water from the well.

All the buildings are made of wood without any nails in them.

This is a bathhouse. It is hot and steamy inside, like a sauna.

Living in Japan

The most powerful people in Japan were fierce warriors called samurai.

Samurai castles were tall, wooden buildings with steep, curved roofs. This is Himeji Castle, near the city of Kobe.

The richest samurai were lords who owned lots of land and lived in big castles.

Warriors and weapons

Each lord had his own army of samurai warriors, who were always ready to fight for him. Some of these warriors were very young – only 13 or 14 years old. Samurai warriors weren't just good at fighting. They also learned how to dance and write poetry.

Here are some samurai warriors with their weapons.

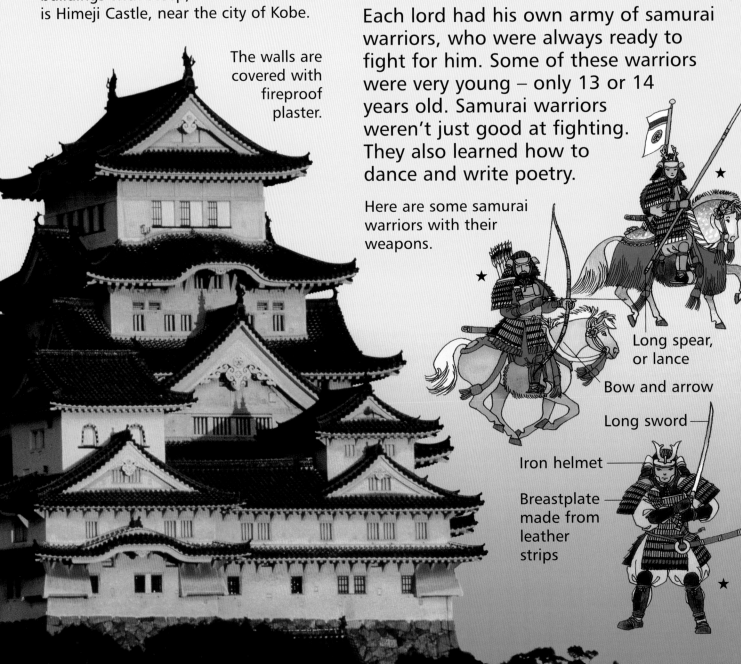

The walls are covered with fireproof plaster.

Long spear, or lance

Bow and arrow

Long sword

Iron helmet

Breastplate made from leather strips

Clothes and customs

Men and women from rich samurai families wore long silk robes, called kimonos. It was against the law for ordinary people to wear silk. Their clothes were made of linen or cotton.

Outside, people wore special shoes to stop their feet from getting muddy. ★

★ In the summer, people carried paper fans and parasols to keep themselves cool.

★ Rich people liked to stroll around in their gardens and admire the scenery.

★ Friends drank tea together in a special ceremony. There were strict rules about how the tea was served.

Internet link

For a link to a website where you can find out more about samurai warriors and print out some fun activities, go to
www.usborne-quicklinks.com

Japanese plays

Rich people in Japan enjoyed watching plays, called Noh plays. All the actors in a Noh play were men, so some of them had to pretend to be women. Noh plays had music, singing, dancing and poetry in them. They were often very sad.

Noh plays are still performed today. The actors wear masks and costumes to show which parts they are playing.

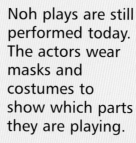

Living in America

In 1620, a group of English people called the Pilgrims, or the Pilgrim Fathers, went to settle in North America. The Pilgrims were very religious. They wanted to be free to worship God in a way they weren't allowed to in England.

The Pilgrims sailed to America on a ship called the *Mayflower*. This is a copy of their ship.

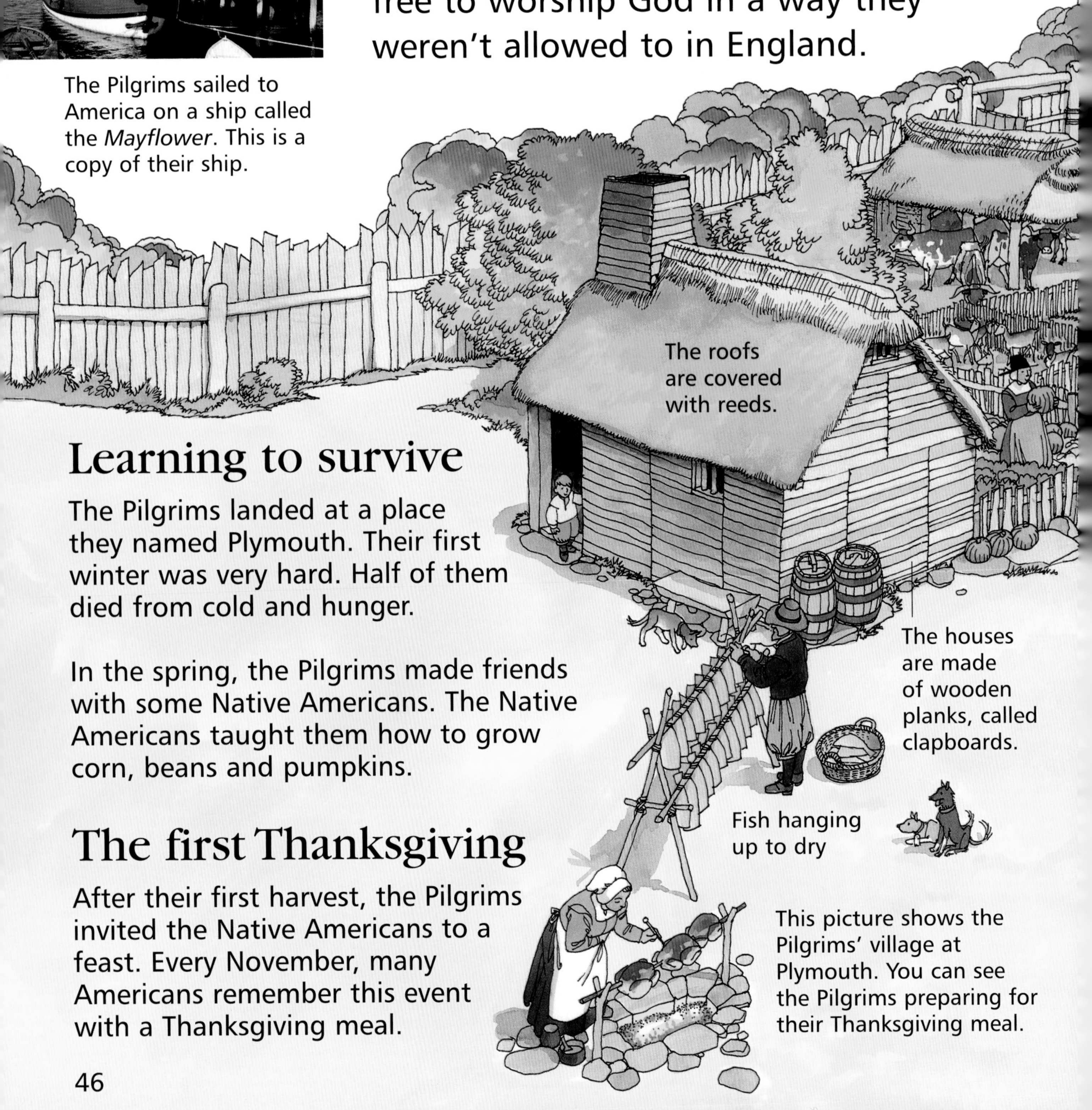

Learning to survive

The Pilgrims landed at a place they named Plymouth. Their first winter was very hard. Half of them died from cold and hunger.

In the spring, the Pilgrims made friends with some Native Americans. The Native Americans taught them how to grow corn, beans and pumpkins.

The first Thanksgiving

After their first harvest, the Pilgrims invited the Native Americans to a feast. Every November, many Americans remember this event with a Thanksgiving meal.

The roofs are covered with reeds.

The houses are made of wooden planks, called clapboards.

Fish hanging up to dry

This picture shows the Pilgrims' village at Plymouth. You can see the Pilgrims preparing for their Thanksgiving meal.

Internet link

For a link to a website where you can explore the Pilgrims' village, go to **www.usborne-quicklinks.com**

This fence keeps wild animals out of the village.

The gardens are planted with beans, onions, turnips and squash.

These women are plucking wild turkeys.

This boy is grinding corn to make bread.

These Native Americans are bringing a deer for the feast.

This woman is stewing pumpkins to put in a pie.

A new country

More and more Europeans came to settle in North America. At first, all the settlers who lived on the east coast of America were ruled by Britain.

In 1783, the settlers won a war against the British and began ruling themselves. They called their new country the United States of America.

This is George Washington, the first President of the United States of America.

Mogul India

At one time, most of India was ruled by Mogul emperors. The Moguls were Muslims who came to India from Central Asia. They were great warriors, but they also loved art, music and poetry.

Mogul buildings

The Mogul emperors were incredibly rich. They used a lot of their money to build beautiful palaces, forts, tombs and mosques (places where Muslims go to worship). Some emperors even built completely new cities.

The walls of the Taj Mahal are decorated with flowery patterns made from over 40 kinds of semi-precious stones.

The most famous Mogul building is the Taj Mahal. It was built by the emperor Shah Jahan as a tomb for his beloved wife, Mumtaz Mahal.

The emperor and his wife are buried in a small underground room beneath the dome.

These tall towers are called minarets.

The Taj Mahal is made of white marble. Over 20,000 builders and artists worked on it.

Palace life

At the emperor's palace, nobles lived a life of luxury. During the day, they strolled in the palace gardens or went hunting. In the evenings, there were great feasts. The guests listened to music and poetry, and were entertained by dancers.

★ A feast at the emperor's palace

The emperor sits on a golden throne.

Musicians

This instrument is called a sitar.

Mogul artists created beautifully detailed paintings. This one shows the emperor Shah Jahan on horseback.

Turban

Veil

Men wear silk gowns, called jama, and leggings, called paijama.

Dancers

Nobles hunted on elephants. They caught fierce animals, such as lions and tigers.

Internet links

For a link to a website where you can see amazing panoramic views of the Taj Mahal, go to **www.usborne-quicklinks.com**

49

Dutch traders

In the 1600s, Holland was a very rich country. Dutch traders, or merchants, owned big ships. They sent their ships all over the world to bring back expensive things to sell.

★ Silk from China

Spices from the East Indies ★

Jewels from ★ India

Here are some luxuries that Dutch traders brought back from overseas.

★ Tea from China

Sugar from Brazil ★

Canal city

The Dutch city of Amsterdam was the busiest port in Europe. Lots of rich bankers and merchants lived there. The city was built around a network of man-made rivers, called canals. Small boats carried goods along the canals to the merchants' homes and storerooms.

This picture shows some merchants' houses in Amsterdam. Part of one house has been cut away to let you see inside.

The houses are very tall and narrow. Some are only 3m (9ft) wide.

Goods are stored in the attic.

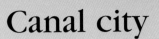
Merchant

This boat is being unloaded.

Floods and flowers

Holland is very flat, and the fields on the coast were often flooded by sea water. Dutch engineers found ways to drain away the water. Farmers used some of this new land to grow flowers from Turkey, called tulips.

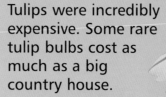

Tulips were incredibly expensive. Some rare tulip bulbs cost as much as a big country house.

Windmills pumped water away from the fields and into canals and rivers.

People displayed their tulips in special vases made from a kind of pottery called Delft.

Popular paintings

The Dutch liked to decorate their homes with beautiful things. Rich merchants paid artists to paint pictures for them. Poorer people could buy pictures from the market. There were even paintings on the walls of bakeries and butchers' shops.

Many Dutch paintings show scenes from daily life. The painting on the left is by an artist named Jan Vermeer.

This woman is going shopping with her maid.

Internet link

For a link to a website where you can watch a video clip about Dutch traders, go to **www.usborne-quicklinks.com**

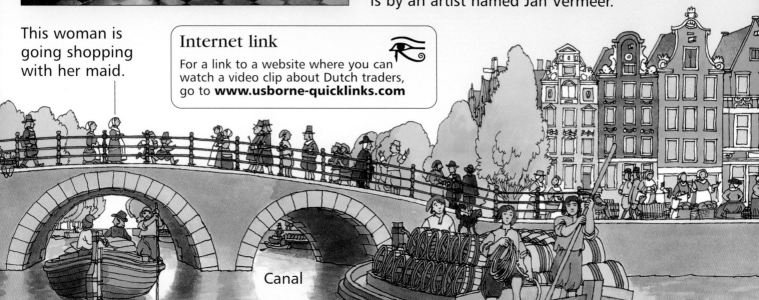

Canal

French finery

Around 350 years ago, the most powerful ruler in Europe was King Louis XIV of France. Louis became king when he was just five years old and he reigned for 72 years. He was fabulously rich and lived a life of luxury.

This is the Hall of Mirrors in the palace at Versailles. One of its walls is covered with 17 huge, arched mirrors.

The king's palace

Louis built a magnificent new palace at Versailles, near Paris. He filled it with priceless furniture, paintings and statues. Louis lived there with his family, his advisers, and over 1,500 servants. Lots of rich French nobles lived in the palace too.

Internet link

For a link to a website where you can look inside the palace of Versailles and explore the gardens, go to **www.usborne-quicklinks.com**

This is Louis XIV's palace at Versailles. It took 47 years to build.

Inside the palace, there are 700 rooms and 67 staircases.

The fountains used so much water they could only be turned on for three hours at a time.

French fashions

In the 1700s, rich nobles at Versailles wore the most fashionable clothes in Europe. Their clothes were made of the finest silk and were decorated with beautiful embroidery, jewels, lace and ribbons.

Here you can see what rich French nobles were wearing in the 1770s.

Men wore wigs made of human, horse or goat hair.

Lace cravat

Silk breeches

Silk stockings

Women had very tall hairstyles, up to 1m (3ft) high.

Rich and poor

In 1789, the poorer people of France rebelled against the rich. They killed the king, the queen and hundreds of nobles, and began ruling the country themselves. This was called the French Revolution.

Some skirts were so wide that women had to go through doors sideways.

The American West

At first, Europeans who settled in North America stayed near the east coast. Then, explorers found ways to the West. Later, families began to cross America looking for land to farm.

Most families started their journey in Missouri, in the United States. These are the routes they took to the West.

This is Chimney Rock, one of the landmarks on the Oregon Trail.

On the move

Families who went to live in the West were called pioneers. They made the long, hard journey in wagons pulled by oxen. Sometimes, they were attacked by Native Americans.

Here you can see some pioneers on their way to the West.

The pioneers have to cross mountains, rivers and deserts.

The wagons are covered with cloth stretched over wooden hoops.

Inside the wagons, there is plenty of food for the journey, as well as farm tools and furniture.

54

Going for gold

In 1848, gold was discovered in California, on the west coast. Thousands of people rushed there hoping to get rich. This was called the Gold Rush.

These men are looking for gold at the bottom of a stream.

★

Internet link

For a link to a website where you can find out more about the Oregon Trail, go to **www.usborne-quicklinks.com**

Farm animals follow behind.

Barrel of water

Lots of families travel together for safety.

Cowboys and cattle

The grassy plains of the West were good for farming cattle. Men called cowboys herded the cattle across the plains. They loaded them onto trains to be sold in the East.

This is what a cowboy wore.

Bandana to keep dust out of his mouth and nose

Lasso for catching cows

Hat with a wide brim

★

Leather leggings, called chaps, to protect his legs

Fighting for land

As farmers moved west, they took land away from the Native Americans who lived there. The Native Americans fought hard to keep their land, but they lost most of it in the end.

This is Sitting Bull, a famous Native American chief.

Victorian times

The time when Queen Victoria ruled Britain is called the Victorian period. By then, there were lots of factories in Britain. Towns grew bigger, as people moved there to work in the factories.

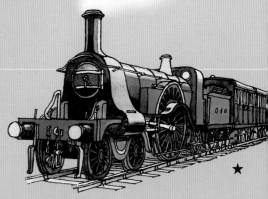

Steam trains like this carried passengers and goods cheaply from town to town.

Living in a town

Rich people owned grand houses at the edge of the town. Factory workers lived in rows of tiny houses, with no running water or inside toilets. The air was full of smoke from the factories, and the streets were filthy. People often got sick and died.

Internet link

For a link to a website where you can travel back in time and visit a Victorian house, go to **www.usborne-quicklinks.com**

Here you can see part of a Victorian town. Can you spot a policeman catching a thief in the street?

Up to 20 people live in each tiny house.

People work long hours in cloth factories like this one.

The streets are lit by gas lamps.

People burn coal to keep warm. Chimneys let out the smoke.

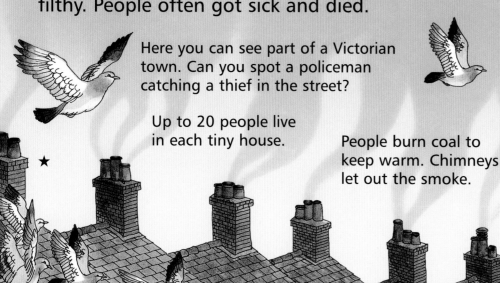

Victorian children

Boys from rich families went to school. Girls were usually taught at home.

Children from poor families had to work in coal mines and factories.

Homeless children were sent to live in a harsh place called a workhouse.

Victorian fashions

In the 1850s and 1860s, women wore dresses with very wide skirts. The skirts were held out by a circular frame called a crinoline. To make their waists look smaller, women wore a kind of tight underwear called a corset.

Victorian women's underwear looked like this.

The ideal waist size was only 45cm (18ins).

Corset

Crinoline

This picture from a Victorian fashion magazine shows what women were wearing in 1859.

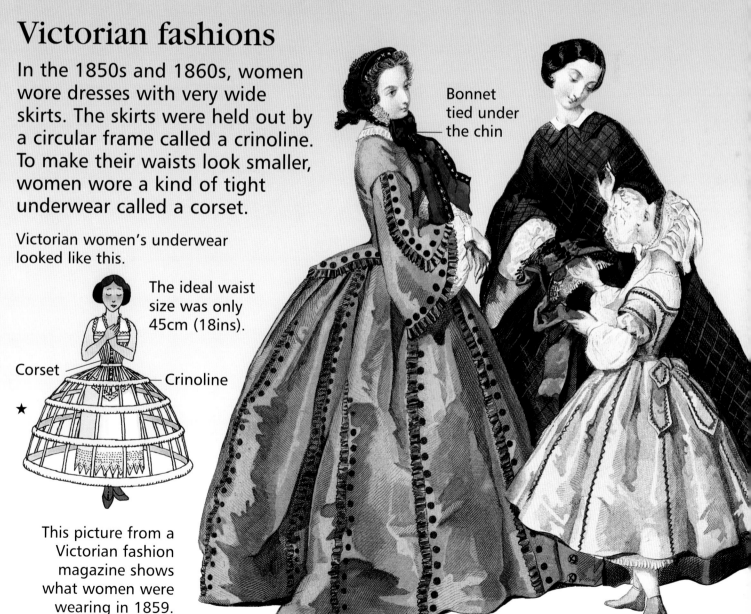

Bonnet tied under the chin

The First World War

The First World War began in 1914. On one side were Britain, France, Belgium and Russia, who were called the Allies. On the other side were Germany and Austria. Later, many other countries joined in too.

The poppies that grew on the battlefields became a symbol for remembering the war.

Internet link

For a link to a website where you can listen to songs from the First World War, go to **www.usborne-quicklinks.com**

In the trenches

A lot of the fighting happened in northern France. Soldiers on both sides dug rows of deep ditches, called trenches, to protect themselves from enemy bullets.

The soldiers lived in the trenches for weeks at a time. During a battle, they climbed out and charged at the enemy. Millions of men died in these terrible battles.

Here you can see some British soldiers in a trench.

The men rest in holes dug into the sides of the trench.

Wooden walkways, called duckboards, stop the soldiers from sinking into the mud.

Officers live in underground shelters, called dug-outs.

The men's feet are always wet and often get sore.

New weapons

Both sides tried new ways of fighting to win the war. The Germans were the first to use poison gas, while the British invented tanks.

German fighter plane

Tanks could run over barbed wire and machine guns, but they often broke down.

German submarines, called U-boats, attacked ships on their way to Britain and France.

Both sides used planes to spy on enemy trenches and to shoot down enemy aircraft.

Soldiers wore masks to protect them from poison gas.

German trench

A soldier called a sentry keeps watch.

Machine gun

Barbed wire

Sandbags

The trenches are full of rats, fleas and lice.

The war ends

In 1917, the United States of America joined the war on the side of the Allies and helped them to win. The war finally ended at 11 o'clock on November 11, 1918. It had killed over 16 million people.

On November 11 every year, many people around the world remember those who have died in wars.

The Second World War

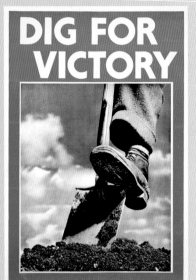

DIG FOR VICTORY

The Second World War started in 1939, when Germany attacked Poland. Later, Japan attacked the United States. Lots of countries joined together to fight the Germans and the Japanese.

There wasn't much to eat during the war. This British poster is telling people to grow their own food.

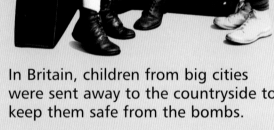

The Blitz

In just a few months, the Germans took over most of western Europe. Then they began bombing cities in Britain. This was called the Blitz. The bombs wrecked buildings and killed thousands of people.

In Britain, children from big cities were sent away to the countryside to keep them safe from the bombs.

Later in the war, the British dropped bombs on German cities. These are the ruins of the city of Cologne.

Internet link

For a link to a website where you can find out what life was like for children in the Second World War, go to **www.usborne-quicklinks.com**

Pearl Harbor

In 1941, Japanese planes attacked American battleships in Pearl Harbor, in Hawaii. The United States joined the war, and the fighting spread to the Far East and the Pacific Ocean.

American soldiers landing on an island in the Pacific Ocean

American ships on fire in Pearl Harbor. Many ships and planes were destroyed or damaged.

The Holocaust

The German leader Adolf Hitler wanted to kill all the Jewish people in Europe. During the war, he had six million Jews murdered. This terrible crime is called the Holocaust.

The war ends

Germany and Japan didn't have enough soldiers or weapons to win the war. The Germans were forced to stop fighting in May 1945.

These Russian soldiers are flying their country's flag in Berlin, the capital city of Germany.

In August, the Americans dropped two huge bombs on Japan. The Japanese finally gave up. The war was over, but it had killed more than 50 million people.

The bombs dropped on Japan were a new kind of bomb, called an atom bomb.

The modern world

On this page, you can read about some of the discoveries and inventions that have changed people's lives since the end of the Second World War.

1952 The first passenger jet began flying.

1957 The first nuclear power station began working in the United States.

1958 The microchip was invented. Microchips are an important part of computers.

1961 Yuri Gagarin was the first person to travel into space.

1962 Live TV pictures were sent from the United States to Europe for the first time.

1967 A doctor named Christiaan Barnard carried out the first heart transplant.

1969 Neil Armstrong was the first person to walk on the Moon.

1969 The jumbo jet flew for the first time.

1972 A game called Pong was the first computer game.

1975 The first home computers were sold in the United States.

This is the space rocket that took Neil Armstrong to the Moon in July 1969.

1976 Concorde began flying. It was the first passenger plane to travel faster than the speed of sound.

1979 The first mobile phones, or cell phones, went on sale in Japan.

1981 The first PC, or personal computer, was made.

1981 The American space shuttle made its first flight.

1982 The first compact discs, or CDs, went on sale.

1982 A patient was given an artificial heart for the first time.

1989 The World Wide Web was invented. The Web allows people to get information from the Internet quickly and easily.

1990 A huge telescope, called the Hubble Space Telescope, was sent into space.

1994 The Channel Tunnel opened between Britain and France.

1997 A sheep called Dolly was the first large animal to be cloned. A cloned animal is an exact copy of another animal.

Index

Picture Credits

Every effort has been made to trace and acknowledge ownership of copyright. If any rights have been omitted, the publishers offer to rectify this in any subsequent editions following notification. The publishers are grateful to the following for permission to reproduce material:

Key: t = top, m = middle, b = bottom, l = left, r = right

Cover, (knight) ©Warwick Castle, (Great Wall of China) ©Michael S. Yamashita/CORBIS; p1, Detail of *August* from *Les très riches heures du Duc de Berry* by Pol de Limbourg/The Art Archive/Musée Condé Chantilly/The Art Archive; p3, ©Archivo Iconografico, S. A./CORBIS; p4b, ©The Natural History Museum, London; p5br, ©The Natural History Museum, London; p7t, ©Gianni Dagli Orti/CORBIS; p7b, George Roos, Peter Arnold, Inc./Science Photo Library; p8tr, ©Copyright The British Museum; p8bl, ©Johnathan Smith/Cordaiy Photo Library Ltd./CORBIS; p10tr, Iraq Museum, Baghdad, Iraq/Bridgeman Art Library; p11tr, ©Copyright The British Museum; p12b, ©Charles & Josette Lenars/CORBIS; p12tr, ©Archivo Iconografico, S. A./CORBIS; p13tl, ©Copyright The British Museum; p13bl, ©Gianni Dagli Orti/CORBIS; p13r, Royal Albert Memorial Museum, Exeter, Devon/Bridgeman Art Library; p14l, ©Angelo Hornak/CORBIS; p14tr, ©Archivo Iconografico, S. A./CORBIS; p16, Fergus O'Brien/Getty Images; p17bl, ©Michael Holford; p19tl, ©Michael S. Yamashita/CORBIS; p19br, ©Keren Su/CORBIS; p20, National Museums & Galleries of Wales; p21mr, ©Roger Wood/CORBIS; p22tl, ©The Vikings, Britain's oldest Dark Age re-enactment society; p23br, Werner Forman Archive/Statens Historiska Museum, Stockholm; p24t (background), ©Digital Vision; p24b, ©Sandro Vannini/CORBIS; p24tr, ©Copyright The British Museum; p25bl, ©Michael S. Lewis/CORBIS; p27tr, The Art Archive/University Library Heidelberg/Dagli Orti; p29tr, ©Michelle Garrett/CORBIS; p29m, ©Gianni Dagli Orti/CORBIS; p29br, ©George McCarthy/CORBIS; p30tl, ©Alan Levy; p30b, Kevin Schafer/Getty Images; p31tl, ©Wolfgang Kaehler/CORBIS; p32tl, Werner Forman Archive/British Museum, London; p34, ©Roger Antrobus/CORBIS; p35ml, *The Annunciation, with St. Emidius,* by Carlo Crivelli/©National Gallery Collection, by kind permission of the Trustees of the National Gallery, London/CORBIS; p35br, Detail from *The Birth of Venus* by Sandro Botticelli/Galleria degli Uffizi, Florence/Photo Scala, Florence; p36-37 (background), ©Digital Vision; p37tr, ©Craig Tuttle/CORBIS; p37br, (astrolabe) ©National Maritime Museum, London; p37tr, (compass) National Maritime Museum, London, UK/Bridgeman Art Library; p38bl, Detail from a portrait of Henry VIII by Hans Holbein/Galleria Nazionale d'Arte Antica, Rome/Photo Scala, Florence; p38tr, ©Adam Woolfitt/CORBIS; p39t, Detail from the Ditchley portrait of Elizabeth I by Marcus Gheeraerts, by courtesy of the National Portrait Gallery, London; p40tl, ©L. Clarke/CORBIS; p41tl, The Art Archive/Topkapi Museum Istanbul/Dagli Orti; p41tr, (porcelain jar and lacquer box) ©Asian Art & Archaeology, Inc./CORBIS; p42tl, Demetrio Carrasco/Getty Images; p42tr, Nationalmuseet, Copenhagen, Denmark/Bridgeman Art Library; p43br, Dave G. Houser/CORBIS; p44, Demetrio Carrasco/Getty Images; p45r, ©Chris Lisle/CORBIS; p46tl, ©Kevin Fleming/CORBIS; p47b, ©Philadelphia Museum of Art/CORBIS; p48tr, ©Elio Ciol/CORBIS; p48b, ©Adrian Pope/Alamy; p49tr, Metropolitan Museum of Art, New York, USA/Bridgeman Art Library; p51ml, *A Gentleman and a Lady Drinking* by Jan Vermeer/Gemäldegalerie, Dahlem-Berlin, Germany/©SuperStock/Powerstock; p51tr, ©Darrell Gulin/CORBIS; p52tr, ©Archivo Iconografico, S. A./CORBIS; p53tr, V & A Picture Library; p55br, ©Bettmann/CORBIS; p57br, Mary Evans Picture Library; p58tl, ©Neil Beer/CORBIS; p59tr, ©George Hall/CORBIS; p60tl, The Imperial War Museum, London; p60mr, ©Hulton-Deutsch Collection/CORBIS; p60b, ©Bettmann/CORBIS; p61tl, ©Bettmann/CORBIS; p61b, ©CORBIS; p62, ©Digital Vision.

Cover design: Andrea Slane
Digital manipulation: Susie McCaffrey, John Russell and Emma Julings
Additional illustrations: David Cuzik and Inklink Firenze

Answer to question on page 7: The cave painting shows a horse, some deer and a bull.